"If you come as softly
As wind within the trees
You may hear what I hear
See what sorrow sees."

~Audre Lorde

First published in India in 2018
by Walking BookFairs
©Walking BookFairs 2018

Cover and Book Design *Biraja Biswal*
Cover Illustration *Sneha Dasgupta*

This edition first published in 2018 by Pan
an imprint of Pan Macmillan Publishing India Private Limited
707, Kailash Building
26, K. G. Marg, New Delhi – 110 001
www.panmacmillan.co.in

Pan Macmillan, 20 New Wharf Road, London N1 9RR
Basingstoke and Oxford
Associated companies throughout the world
www.panmacmillan.com

ISBN 978-93-86215-40-6

Walking BookFairs, HIG-34, Phase I
Khandagiri, Housing Board Colony
AMRI Hospital Road, Bhubaneswar
Odisha – 751030

Printed and bound in India by
Replika Press Pvt. Ltd.

100

POEMS
ARE NOT
ENOUGH

To
bookshops
and
booksellers
of
the
world
and
the
bare
hands
that
create
books
for
all
to
read.

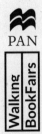

CONTENTS

Da Vinci
Of The Wilds
—*Abubakar Adam Ibrahim*

Write beautiful poetry, they say.
Write of blooming gardenias and
Flushed orchids,
Of sparkly springs that tickle,
Of green hills and flowered fields,
Of lions in the wild and safaris.
Write of culture and refinement, they say.
Of the arts and the maestros,
Of Da Vinci and Mona Lisa,
Of Michelangelo and David,
Of Mozart and the symphonies!
But who is this Da Vinci
Compared to our precocious brood,
Maestros before they could wear shoes,
Painting lavishly;
Blood on clouds,
Gore on foliage?
Does David compare to their works
Of sculpturesque ribs, gutted mountains,
Bloody rivers, bloated cadavers?
Do the symphonies compare to
Their melodies
Of shattering, crunching, booming,
Wailing, plunking, popping,
Pitter-pattering,
Silence?
Never mind they never thanked you
For the tools of their arts;
The ordinance
Words get stuck in their throats now.
But they will thank you when
They are older.
You just wait and see
My friend, your story is of snowflakes
And sunny morns.
Mine is of slugflakes, chains,
Jackboots, razor wires
It is coloured by fire and desolation,
Sometimes blotched by little laughters.
Our poetry is our story
And this
I will write.

Nallamma
—Iniyavan Banumathi

Nallamma's decaying limbs and the tapioca
She bred spoke equally of her resistance.

Once an exotic poetry loving white lady
Asked Nallamma to describe her orgasm.

"Odour of endosulfan wouldn't give me one"
She's no goddess.

To conceal her embarrassment and avert
Collapse, a pair of shoes for her
Distorted feet is
All that Nallamma needs.

Not your superlatives.

Nallamma never taught her kids self respect.

She just took them for a mile walk over the
Ploughed fields where she refined her
Tumbling Steps, let them see her breast feed
Her frail Co-worker's infant, and
The daily war she Waged against
Patriarchs for her harvest-share,
Survival and self-respect.

To cook dinner after sunset is blasphemous
Nallamma told her children.

They grew up to find amma served them
Food Cold for it is less consumed.

They survived. All of them.
She's not a painting, a poem or
An anthropology research material.
You can't dissect her wounds.
You can't exhibit her shadows.
You can't confine her
To your arthouses and laboratories.
She ain't surreal.
She's an intense reality.
Nallamma is a tapioca farmer.

The Letter

—Pankaj Sekhsaria

Who knew my address,
To write me a letter?

The envelope and a small
Piece of paper inside.

No date…no name,
Only six lines of vagabonds
And loneliness.

Or was it about a journey
And about me?

Who will write to me
About vagabonds but her,

Who will write to me
About journeys but her,

Who will write to me
About loneliness?

She is my other woman…

Writing about her love for me?

Or,

Or is it her final goodbye…?

Diamonds

—Easterine Kire

I don't like
Diamonds Satabdi
Something hard
About diamonds
Something cold
Razored stalactites
I think of the men
Who rip out the stone
Their hands grimy
With unnecessary soil
I think of the men
Who grind the stone
The harshness
Of that sound
Rock against stone
Sharp
Shrill
Shriek
Shattering the quiet
In taut lines
I never liked it
When my daughter
Dropped
The crystal bowl
So it sharded into
A million diamonds
Crystal diamonds
Glittering in corners
Awaiting their turn
To be swept up
Crystal diamonds
That cut my finger
When I thought
I had picked up
The last gleaming
Never liked diamonds
Never.

Forbidden

—Soumyadeep Bhattacherya

God made me but
You didn't accept me;

From every sector
We are abolished,

Thrashing away
Like a wrecked piece.

I am forced to do this,

As nobody accepted me as it is.

Selling my body
I earn a living,

Quotes are buried down
With no meanings.

I wonder, why people
Say such things,

When it looks alluring
Only in pricey coverings.

I have no objections but,

Do not inject
Any false impression.

I have lost all hopes;

Pleading that future
Not follow,

Ultimately, heart's beating
With inner sorrows.

Blessings
From The Infinite
—Tania Dey

He looks at me
Without batting an eyelid
At my large doe eyes
My brown lips
And my thinning arms and stature

His fingers trace
First my wrinkled skin,
My ruffled hair
And exposed collar bone.

He once gazed at me the same way
When we lay under the sycamore;
Hands entwined
And hearts interlaced
Eyes reflecting the constellations
That lay betwixt us.

Those eyes reminded me of river currents
One caused another to ripple
Until the physical being shook
Alerted at being struck,
Much like the high notes on a piano.

Love rekindled,
After a decade;
And I feel pansies and daises grow
Where once my dead soul was housed.

An infant's cry interrupted our moment
She raised her arms
Demanding affection
And my husband cradled
Our daughter.

Here Again
—Sristi Suman

I want to tell you
A secret today.
It is about the
Four summer days
When I picked a clover
And turned back
On the field, and saw him
In radiance.
I want to tell you that
I fell in love...
The summer,
The Sun, the light,
That the clover crumpled
In my hands, fell
When he pulled the
Ribbons and ran
And I was stunned
By the wind he left me in.
I want to tell you that
I've walked under the meadows
With him holding
Stray branches
At bay for me
The rains, the drips, the wet grass,
And I have turned
And laughed
For the follies of his
That didn't hit the mark.
I want to tell you that
I've closed my eyes
And waited, when he was
Fixing up the lights
The dark,
The search, the touch,
That I've watched
Him sleep,
When he hid like
Someone scared.
I want to tell you
How we parted,
That it was the closest breath
After that first night
The smell,

The hold,
The taste,
That it lasted for no time
And I am tracing
It ever since.
I want to tell you this secret
About a four day summer love
That it was then and it is now
That it still meets me today.
But I want to tell you
This secret today
Because this summer
You're here,

Again, and you're
Forty and battered,
Because you've come looking.
Because it's just summer
And the rains are coming.
Because the field is a step away
And the lights are going to fade,
Because you're here again,
And we haven't moved
From here since then.

Love Bites
—*Kuntala Sengupta*

It would be easy
Berry picking like,
I know you think.
To own me,
With your flair,
The same effortlessness
With which you once
Disowned me.
For all such times
When I sizzled in your arms
Red chilli on hot mustard oil,
I gave you flavour,
Burning myself down.
You separated the torment,
Knowing its destiny,
Down in the bin.
But here it rises,
Fiery, flaming,
In words,
Bleeding words.
Does that hurt you?
The burning red wound?
Not yet?
Good.
It decided to let you go,
No, not because it cannot,
I cannot.
But I know,
It's not worth.
Your pain.
You are a destitute,
A lonely tree,
In your palatial backyard.
You could not house
My blooming births.
And on an other day,
When you are disowning
Someone else,
I wish her the strength
Of dried chillies,
And buried flowers,
To burn you down.

In love,
And its beautiful
Helplessness.
In hate,
And its terrible
Helplessness.

We Speak For
Our Journey
—Avishek Bhattacharjee

Dust smells of a bright day
Sun-ray speaks and
Chillness hold
Freedom clings to the body..
Waiting for the sunset
One glass of rawness
And time is sold

The ubiquitous smell of vile
The game of love and hate is on
Lesson was for survival
Blood is no more a myth to smile

Roads look new but
The journey is known

Wash your hands and
Start the day
Of the wicked closet
Or the clingy heart

The path you travel has
No name of its own

Nothing in vain as the
Color we sight
Blood,race and valor
Listen to the whistle..
You need to start
Time has come to witness
The battle of pride and might.

If I Must
—Unika Prusty

I am not buried under
The debris of a broken image.

My head is still sticking out,
My eyelids still fluttering
Searching for yet another
Landscape to paint,
Yet another horizon to fly.

I would indeed embody
The last phoenix, if I must!

For, there still are songs to sing
There still are colours to emerge...

Emerge from this symphony
Of breath, this chaos of being
This soul-stirring salsa
Of yours and mine.

Breath by breath,
Rhythm by rhythm,
Scar by scar
We will put together
The pieces of a life
And colour it with our blood.

If Once More
—*Anupam Patra*

If I once more were to
Have you lying by my side
Like the very first time, from where,
To live the rain kissed zephyr,

You had walked and
Split the curtains
Letting the sky and
Clouds see us in their cloth

If you once more were
To be alone with me in the woods
When the fawn scampered
To your feet

And you playfully fed it the crumb
And led it to let you kiss its nose

If you once again walked
Close by me
Leaning on my shoulder
And seizing my arm

Our hopes melting
And dreams marrying

The way you were letting me
Conceal you from me
And sometimes from yourself

And we had tread on sun dried maple
Whose sighs, breaking
Under your fragile steps

Had mended our fears &
Bridged our souls

If you were to raise those to life
Just, once more,
I promise I'll be gone
And of you I'll ask nothing more

Over Again
—Harendera Chauhan

Over Again

This seems like
Never again

Last time when
We touched pain

Those winters of
Shared coffee and wine

How together we followed
The sunshine?

We had a pool of dreams,
A river of life.

Flowing perennial
Down in our hearts

Providing seasons to us
Oh! How I thought
This will never be again?

Now you are coming a new
After long dark nights
Fresh like a dew
Afraid is me so must be you
We had a goodbye,
Now we will have a kiss too.
Over again
You have come to me
Bringing spring

Bygone Longing
—Prajyoti Pati

I loved you with every breath
I cared you with every beat
You thought I damned you
Every moment I'd never been
With you for a tick You left
Me in the mid air I mastered
Myself to survive You asked
Me to leave you I wanted the
Past to be revived You went
Stubborn I loved the
Accusations You finally
Dumped me And I lived an
Austere life I closed my
Lashes and saw you lying on
The grass You gave no
Thought of coming back
And I was forever thwacked.

Crafty

—Louise Kowitch

Profane, irreverent,
You don't care
You take a bus
Without the fare

Upend my world
Send up a flare

And in the end
It seems unfair

With every sunset
You trespass

Drifting through
The island pass

I lack the will,
I act so crass

I chase you down,
Betray my class.

So once again that
Orange sky
I watch it from
12 stories high

It signifies what you deny

A dream that
Fades into goodbye

Persistence is
My only craft.

Being Lucky
—*Anurag Sahoo*

I got this feeling of being lucky
When I buy fried chicken of Kentucky
I have money which I can spend
On the cool gadgets and the latest trend
I am glad to get a job to earn money
I don't have to rob
I am lucky because I have a family
Who cares for me and loves me daily
But still I weep and complain for more
I wish for a house with Maple wood floor
Still I want to ride a luxury sedan
And to wear Swiss watches and suits Italian
Now let's take a look at the other side of this story
Which will disapprove my above theory?
Where I eat lobsters which taste so good
There are people who struggle to get some food
While I spend thousands in movies and popcorn
There are people whose dresses are tattered
And torn
Just when I was angry due to office
And its grind
I saw a person with a stick as he was blind
I always shave using the fragrant foam
And browse Internet with Google chrome
But there are people who pick rags and roam
And return to a tent which they call their home
It is then I realize that the majority is poor
For them, even a square meal is grandeur
While I think about getting higher education
They wait in the queue to get some ration
This is a story of two worlds apart
By every sense it will break our heart
Time to realize how lucky we are
And praise the God and thank our star
Don't worry about the rising cost of living
Rather be kind and feel the joy of giving
There is no reason for us to be coarse
As people have problems which are probably worse
Try to appreciate the things you have
Never be greedy to commit a big gaffe
Life may not end up like the way we dream
But we should always remain happy
And content.

Moon

—*Ankita Kanungo*

I knew it was time;
To meet someone
Who was always mine.

The werewolf roared;
My tattered wings soared.
The strong wind held me back;
The clouds made sure
I lost my track.

Shattered and broken,
I fell down;

Silver light covered me up
Like a gown.
He shone and I reminded him
Of his breach;
I knew he was the love
I wouldn't ever reach.

Back Then
—*Bagmita Mishra*

Back then,
I was five when,
Mom said over and over again;
I was a precious gem!
Winning hearts time and time again
Which was back then!

Back then,
I was a teen when,
Dad said, all English channels forbidden,
Which made my heart dishearten.
Scary stories, sure did frighten.
Jolly-merry celebrations,
Of course did happen.
Ah! That was back then!!

Back then,
I was young when,
Days were shiny golden,

Salman Khan; gosh left me smitten.
At times all worries forgotten.
Daring dishonesty also forgiven.
All these; back then!

Back then,
Created memories a dozen.
Not a moment barren.
A journey, never to be forsaken.
Priceless smiles, all god-given.
Learnt lessons to enlighten.
It was, back then.

Dharma
Is A Black Cat
In A Dark Room
—Ankita Das

You see a pair of eyes watching
You in the dark.

Your heart starts to race, your mind
Is filled with terror

You stop moving when the creaking of the
Chair adds to that eerie feeling

You can almost feel the brooding
Presence of the creature

As it starts to scratch it's nails,
You are left with goose bumps

You feel like a criminal,
Helpless you decide to surrender

You bow before the creature,
As an attempt to wash away the sins

Filled with guilt, you cry and beg

Begging for mercy, you fear
The punishment awaiting you

You start to pray, pray out fear

Eyes shut down, you are on your knees

Suddenly you are shaken up by a noise

You almost choked, as your heart leapt
Out of your chest

Ready to face the inescapable
Gathering all the courage that's left
You open your eyes

The room's filled with light
The creatures gone, there's not another soul
And all that's left is the empty milk bowl.

Unfinished Thoughts
—Sourav Panda

Hope is a seven-storey building;
Taller, if you are a poet.
Jump off from there,
And mankind is killed.
The thoughts that must have passed
The dimly lit station of his mind
That morning, shall always be moving,
Undefined, undecided and unfinished.
In an endeavor to attain freedom,
A man was killed.
He must have thought of
His favorite comic,
And the bitter sip of rum.
He must have thought about
His favorite movie and
His red-stained report card.
In an attempt to fly, a man was killed.
He must have thought
Of his clean bed sheets,
His heart breaks, and the lost cause
Of legalizing marijuana in his country.
And for the sake of love, a man was killed.
When you decide to die,
You are dead already; sometimes twice.
And then he must have thought
Of his favorite cigarette
And his father's persistent cough.
He must have tried to recall the freshness
Of his favorite poetry on life
And the fading spot of blood
On his favorite shirt.
For the lack of pain, a man was killed.
He could not probably recall God
And must have thought
About his pet instead.
He must have thought of watering
The plants in his room,
One last time.
In his attempt to live, a man was killed.
Somewhere in a dimly lit station,
A man is dead, maybe twice, already.

A Verse Finds
An Admirer
—*Nrapen Sipani*

A verse finds an admirer.
A heart finds it's soul.
An illusion of love for beauty
And 'the beauty' of the well.

From the feeling of attraction,
Through the lane of lust,
Till the taste of valour,

Every feeling, enslaved by the sheer urge
Of achieving perfection.

The sister Ugly is lost,
No love for her, just the disgust.
Disgust is 'attraction in disguise' .

It comes after Beauty's demise.
A chance for disgust to rule out beauty,
As if like establishing it's virtue,

Like a blow on the malleable metal shell.
Disgust with every blunt hit,
Shapes the soul in its own reflection.
With existing virtue springs out as sparks.
Disgust unlike his cousin adjectives,

Is not relative.
A warning to keep us safe,
As a natural survival instinct.
So, it must not be relative.
But we lose the chance,
To be free.

As, we remain divided at our disgust.
Our delusion of awareness stays.
Our gray made us superior,
But we choose to remain hypocrites.

Rainbows, Faded
And Still Unchased
—Soumyajit Pradhan

Wearing the robes of mystics
Ascetics, cloaked in penance
For sins unknown of lives past.

Dream, we did; dare too
Of owning the world, reigning
Kingdoms, littered with stardust.

Our slates, once sparkling clean
Now much used, overwritten
Dusted and wiped, time and again
Have finally lost their sheen.

Our lives, once hopefully naive
Dreams, pure and brave
Now much ruined, overwhelmed
Rainbows, faded and still un-chased.

Hanging By A Dream
—Priyanka Rath

With a sliver of light,
Comes wrapped a little dream,
Burning steadily in my eyes.

Through chaos, stillness and
Lost moments,
The dream surges:
Chanting, fear not, hide not,
Undefeated yet, many roads
Await you, yet.

When my voice of doubt is the loudest,
Drowning me in erasure,
It goads me to break chains,
To believe in the infinite magic
Of the cosmos.

It resonates, like a familiar song,
At times, like a faint strain of
A smile forgotten,
It wakes by my sleep.

Today is the tomorrow you
Awaited yesterday,
My dream says.
Till the last breath, dream.

Miracles In The Mundane

—Sheetal Mehta

What is light?
Not in the brightest of daylight,
But in the pitch black darkness of life.
Where I stumble, I fall;
Not even courageous to crawl,
Afraid of the shadows in me, after all.
And that's where my miracle lies.
For how could there be a shadow,
If there wasn't;
Somewhere deep within me,
A hidden light shining bright.

What is a story?
Not mentioned in an elaborated classic,
But on the fields of war,
Where I endlessly fight the odds;
Sometimes I win, but today I lost,
And as I close my eyes, for once and all,
I witness my miracle call.
For how could my story be ending;
When I'm still alive,
In those thousand content smiles,
I saved with each breath of mine.

You talk about Miracles?
What I see is enough.
What fills these eyes,
Plenty.

If I Could Eat
The Air Over
The Everest
—*Saluvi Prasad*

What do I do, in a world full of you?
You, who disagrees to agree,
With every thought that is free,
Freedom to say or convey,
To care or not to care,
To own that space in the world,
Where I can write my name in bold,
To break that mold of me,
To be and just let be,
To ride on the smoke of a bike,
Then fly hinged to a kite.
Type, retype and erase,
That which I dislike in a phase,
Or nothing at all yet in a zest,
I could eat the air over the Everest.

The Unwritten Letter

—Anindita Deo

Tonight I think
Of what I was
To you, and to myself.
I empty my pockets. A torn ticket,
A candy wrapper, two coins,
A carefully folded paper,
Moist along the creases.
Thumbing the lines
You had scribbled,
I touch you
With my charred finger.
Uttering the words,
Smudged and wet
I bleed ink from my mouth.
Tonight I think
Of what I was
To you, and what I must
Write to you from
A strange town,
Submerged in
Spiteful rain.
Do I tell you where have I been,
In the alleys of dusk,
The mountains of dust?
Do I tell you what I felt,
Even if I don't remember
Much at all?
Your questions lie cold,
Seeking the warmth
Of answers,
Or the solace of
Tepid excuses.
Words flutter,
But won't alight
I trace their dim trail
In the cold night
And wonder if I get to keep
All the goodbyes
I won't get to use.

Children
—Nicole Nies

Children,
Let's give them
A bright future
By saving the earth
Today.

Romance

—Jash Sen

Romance is insipid
So much more zest in a voice
As it yells
In a well aimed kick
As it fills
The armchair
From its rest.
Who needs to play cupid?

Star Dust
—Cipun Mishra

I read somewhere
90% of us is stardust;
But we shut our eyes
To celestial chatter.
We are impatient people.

We lament where we are,
While we struggle
To know who we are.
We could channel energies,
Silence musical chaos,
But we are impatient people.

You write poems
On your skin,
Like plastic flowers.
There is art in pretense,
A certain flair
You could almost see.
How color blind are we to dreams?
Promising hearts,
Like they were empty jars,
We survived cracks
These faltering lies tell.

You could live through
Heartbreaks, but
We are impatient people.

Delimit

—*Sohela Chhotaray*

Human emotions are chaotic,
Stammered hopes,
Withered dreams,
For which my myness is shivering.
It should be observed like, mean,
Median or mode, like maths or logic,
Like waxing and waning
Of the moon,
Or to be biased like the blind
Belief of love.
I unfurled the past,
Which made me rethink of caste,
Creed and religion,
For a matured social life,
With scared heartbeats, which we
Used to believe in our schooldays..
Untouchability, taboos,
Social expectations, etiquette's are
To be considered, what we inherited
From generations, but rarely given
A second thought.
Now it appears like a nightmare,
I have forgotten, the world of
Dominance and recessive,
The axe and the tree,
The rule of the jungle,
I thought this is Utopia,
But Alas!! Pandora's box was open,
Before the birth and rebirth,
So why sob?
Why complain?
Practice, prejudice or prediction
Would not work, but
Bliss or Omen works,
Even if we have surrendered..

Self Love

—Sweta Mishra

Thick branches hide the
Overgrown petals,
Sleeping between ferns, are desires.
To touch them, is wrong, you say?
Fear is holding my branches back
From feeling the warm home inside me,
The petals,
Between the ferns.

Sunset eyes go dim, go dark.
My branches reach out to the ferns,
The petals
Life returns.
I float
In the bowls of my petrichor.
Slipping, dripping,
Staining the sheets

No, I will not. I will not abide
By your rules.
Yes, I will. I will feel this softness,
This strength.
Scared, are you?
Fullness of my flesh,
Does not need you.

Clitoral, vaginal, blooming fantasies,
Pleasures and awakening.

Half A Woman

—Ankita Sahoo

The window swings open
The tender dawn breeze tickling her bare toes.
Her body felt unknown under the covers,
Yet somebody was celebrated in the soul.
The antique mirror refuted her
Budding womanhood
And so did the old clock on the wall.
Each one cautiously reminding her
Of the identity she was assigned by the world.
Hesitant still, she gives in to the
Morning's gentle tug
And gracefully ballets out of bed.
With half opened eyes, humming
A favorite tune
Smelling the scent of roses so red.
And like a freedom break granted
In a life time of silent confinement.
She drifted away into her secret kingdom
Where every desire had wings.
She swung her hips from side to side
And grooved with tender feet.
She bathed in aroma and played
With the bubbles
And slipped into sophisticated silks.
A stroke of red on lips, soft pink on cheeks
Mom's stolen treasures find homage.
A hidden wig resting behind
The dusty cupboard
Now proudly crowning her head.
A wide smile spreading across her face
A twinkle sparkling in her eyes.
She relived the soul under her body
The old mirror still orthodox to acceptance.
Knock, knock, knock.
Loud knocks religiously hammered the door.
"Your breakfast is ready," said the voice
From the other side.
The smell of strong coffee slowly floating
In to the room.
Off came the wig, the silks, the red
Stripping naked the woman inside.
Suit on, boots on.

The heavy musk cologne replacing
The sweet fragrance.
Her manly anatomy barred her
To revel in her womanly bliss.
In a man's world she was a man
Uncomfortable, misfitting but still a man.
A drop of tear ran down her cheeks
"Chin up, Princess!" said she to the half
Woman in the mirror.
I will return to my kingdom victoriously
After defeating the demons of the day
Lurking Outside...the other end of the door.

After Her Visit Home
—*Yogesh Maitreya*

Lately she blossomed
In the season of womanhood.
Except her name,
She has no relationship with Allah.
I, since my childhood,
Have been drinking the bitter peg
Of the truth that said,
"Ambedkar and the Buddha are
Human beings"
And became a Kafir.
I asked her, "Do you offer Namaz?".
"No" she answered, without understanding
The purpose of my question.
In that morning of drizzle
As our bodies touched each others,
We transformed into human beings.
But one day she went back home
And started telling me about Moharram.
After that day she did not return,
Perhaps, she understood
The purpose of my question.

Regret

—Saumya Subhra Samantaray

For the person who was
Everything to me,
For the person I regarded
As my friend for life,
I was just another woman.

For all the prayers, for all the hope,
For all the dreams and tales,
Stabbing was the only answer.

Feelings don't flow in a single way,
I couldn't have missed the linking road.
I know it existed somewhere,
Lost amidst your words,
Lost in the distance,
Lost amidst the lights, the brightness
In your world.

Let the lights be on, spirits be high,
Prayers get answered,
Happiness prevail.
Time will heal it all.

Just Not Tonight
—Sanchita Dwivedi

What is the night made of?
If not broken stars
And edgy shards of
Dreams and hearts,
Glued together by
The moon up there,
And courage in my eyes.
Leave me alone,
Under this patch of life.
I will be fine, just not tonight.
What is the night made of?
If not the nomadic clouds
And cruel silence hovering
Over the moonlit roofs
Held together by
The sparkling stream
And tears in my eyes.
Leave me alone
In this rain of woe.
I will be fine, just not tonight.
What is the night made of?
If not the lone leaf
And lifeless white branches of ivy,
Swaying alone;
Bound still by
The symphony of nature
And screams of my soul.
Leave me alone,
Behind this veil of chaos.
I will be fine, just not tonight

Strangers
—Ro Hith

We meet; two silent landscapes.
Intimacies, hidden waters,
Lost in the speed of details.

I wave my hand; The slowness
Of a wall clock in an abandoned home.
She smiles; A smile measured secretly
In the excess of togetherness.
A letter never meant to be read
Enveloped in our indifferent gazes.

We stay still; like a moment between
Two trains, crossing.

The two trains part,
Our seats exchange.

War

—Anshuman Dash

We are at war.
A war with ourselves,
A war with the world
A war without a beginning,
A war without an end
A war without a reason
A war without amends
A war for religion
A war for race
A war with the universe
A war to find our place
We are at war.
A war with the living
A war with the dead
A war over water
A war over bread
A war for blood
A war for scars
A war for peace
A war for wars
A war with nature
A war with men
A war to survive
Just to die again
We are at War.

Making Love
—Madhumoy Satpathy

His fingers kissed the keys.
Maddened by passion
They were making love now.
Wild passionate love
They moaned sweetly

Wanting to love something, someone
I loved the keys that night
And wrote this poem.

Lobster Dreams
—Pintu Bhattacharjee

You see people dancing,
Hoarding, haggling
Why?
Why do we react to screams?
Why?
Why wails wake us up?
And not individual scores of teardrops.

Have you ever felt the pangs within?
Of all the flickering lights
Adorning billboards
Or of the empty measured distances
Among houses in the neighborhood
Or, is it only me?

What are we selling?
What are we buying?
What are all the debates about?
All day long

Soullessness? Inequalities?
Will apocalypse make us realize?
So, the inertia of surging ahead runs
Until a point of no return,
No replenishing the resources already spent

Read, learn, find,
New studies and statistics
Yet no stopping your splurges
And people who witness and
Validate this are at the
Top of all debauchery.

Remedy?
Solidarity, compassion, fraternity, unity?
Horse shit, a huge façade.
And now I return to my own high spirits
And I call it all
Lobster Dreams.

I Compete With Me

—*Anup Padhi*

Running through the meadow and
Jumping on the hay
I start with some beautiful moments
Of my childhood days
From childhood to adulthood
Moments flow like a stream
Sailing in this stream I craft my dreams

These dreams are distant, the path is foggy
I start my journey with the rising sun
With tiny dots in the empty horizon
Connecting these dots I make a path
Sometimes I win sometimes I lose
But this journey gives me courage
My dreams are limitless just like the sky
Opening up my arms I try to hug them
With my eyes
From the moment I am born
Till the moment I die
Where I just compete with 'Me'.

Sometimes They Appear
—*Chaitra Hegde*

There are these things on my neck , face, ear,
Even on my penis, rarely, but yes sometimes.
Smooth, round shiny with a white head red
Projecting out like a bump raising proudly
They come up in 2-3 days, usually
I try to pop Them take the life out of them.
They refuse, I fight sometimes they give up,
Vomit the venom, the white life out of their
Mouth and a little blood out of their
Little hearts a bump full of life that I had felt
With my Fingertips a few hours back.
They lie there, Dead, limp or infuriated,
Inflamed a bigger, redder, hotter bump.
I live with them either way, either carrying
A corpse on me, for next Few hours or days,
Making sure it is dead, now and then.
And then they live on like scars on
My face limb wherever for rest of their lives
Telling their own story in difference to mine
Shouting out in fact and I live on in constant
Fear ready to close their gaping scar of
A mouth whenever I encounter you.
Strangely, it has never occurred to me that
Perhaps I should leave them alone leave them
To go away on their own without leaving
A trace. I am sure a few must have vanished
Like that without me noticing. I disapprove.
I shudder at the very thought of life
Disappearing under me without me
Even noticing! Sometimes they appear.

Hold On

—Nipunya Panda

Faith is amorphous,
Yet, hold on.

We have stood,
Bowed-down to the
Storm-clouds above,
And hardships have rained
All this while.
Running away has been
Hard-fought;
Faith is amorphous.

Adversities have been traps,
Like a huge labyrinth,
With tunnels made of fire that are
Closing in on us,
Escaping is just fiction;
We're prisoners of
A holocaust of despair,
Bailing out is a hopeless premise;
Oh, faith has been amorphous.

But, be that as it may,
Hold on;
Hold on for the pearl
Is about to take shape,
Take shape out of the sea of
Tears that the Oyster has shed.
Hold on, for your shine would
Show the light of the day;
The dusk is melting away
Into the break of dawn,
Hold on.

When
—*Agantuk*

When a year seems too long and
Starts to haunt –
Think of the falling leaf month,
The chilly winter January,
The bright leaves of spring.

When a month seems too long and
The future dreary –
Think of the floating clouds on a blissful day,
The morning cuckoo singing a hymn to thee,
The afternoon moon peeping behind
The peepul tree.

When a day seems too long and
Starts to wither –
Think of the minutes of darkness
Breaking into daylight,
The wee hours after the twilight
Colours linger,
The silence of midnight.

When a minute seems too long
And gathers dust –
Think of the passing seconds of the hour hand,
The whistle of a train far out,
The dying breath.

When a second seems too long and
Unimportant –
Think of the moment you looked lovingly
Towards each other,
The vision of the past and future together.
When at last the moment comes-
Think of the time you had
In between giving in and giving out.

Dr. Ambedkar
—*Ramu Ramanathan*

Lalji
Travelled many miles
From Champaner
To Mumbai
In silence
He paid obeisance
At the memorial in Dadar
On 6 December
Although
He could not read or write

Lalji
With his meagre savings
Purchased eleven books that had Doctor
Saheb on the cover
He
Returned home
Didn't eat on the train
Determinedly
Clutched the eleven books
Which his three daughters
Would read, again and again
For a year
Till the next anniversary of Doctor Saheb
On 6 December

Of Men And Musicians

—Shruti Kulkarni

Their music
Sound of a gentle churning
In the deepest part
Of the earth.
We love them
For their unkempt sideburns
And cigarette smells.
Their laughter echoing
Unfiltered white-noise
To complement warblers' ruckus
Trombone to forest song.
We love them
For the careless 'unbuttoned-ness' of shirt,
Yet subtly proclaiming gentlemanliness.
Their banter
Poetry midst the prose of life
Streaks of bright red in monochrome.
We love them
For their coffee-stained teeth
Yet an unfettered smile breaking between
A mustache and a beard.
Their weathered face
Maps of places we want to travel to
But the eyes is where we want to build a home.

When Night Falls
—*Vinutha Mallya*

This Night is in me.
This night and all those –
Hidden in their every shade
The cries of battered voices.
The Grey Night is in me.
Howling beasts and dazzling fireflies
Meandering; drowning
Beaten screams from weak bodies.
The Ebony Night is in me.
Tropical trees droop, exhausted
By heat; waiting
For the dust to wrap their prey.
The Black Night is in me.
Its soundless hush
Unbroken, long; laying
Death at my door.
This Night is in me.
Today and every day –
Wars and epics written
Here, where my heart keeps beating.

Giving Love
A Bad Name
—Raghavendra Madhu

Nature can barely damage our numb lives;
We are disease, nature is cure.
Take two bowls of conversations,
One bowlful of Donyi, one bowlful of Polo,
Sprinkle some takar, weed the domey,
Ensure to keep the dogum dor,
Wrap it in an oko leaf warmed in fire,
Stuff it in a uddu, fill to the brim with poka,
Put it in a lichik on high flames, let it shimmer
And fill the room with a Galo dream.

Dreams take time to weave itself
Like a kaleidoscopic gale with forests,
And animals prints on it.
The weaver keeps human traces out.
It is reasonable to be scared;
The human design could fade the others,
Giving love a bad name.
I wonder who reads Erepthela
For the vanishing wild.
Togo tells me, if you are dying in pain,
Confession could ease your pain.
Confession is sedative;
Sedative is peace and to die
Peacefully is a great thing.

*(Note: The Galo are a central Eastern Himalayan tribe
which primarily inhabit the West Siang district of Arunachal
Pradesh.*

*Donyi:Sun/ Polo:Moon/ Donyi Polo:Religion/ Takar:Stars
/ Domey:Clouds / Dogum Dor:Thunder / Lichik:Fire place
/ Uddu:A bamboo utensil / Poka:Local rice beer /
Gale:Long piece of cloth worn around the waist by women/
Erepthela: Galo Hymns for the dead)*

A Boy
Named Shoo!
—Rishav Dave

The sun burns with
An ironsmith's ardor,
Those stuck in this big ball of heat
Limp to the shadows,
And stick to them.
But not Shoo!
For the bright sun is the only one
Who burns with love for him.
He hears them murmur as he
Slithers away from them,
"Stay away from him.
He is not human," warns one.
"Oh what a gift from the gutters,"
Someone mutters.
"Shoo! Stay away!"
Orders another.
"And they call the sun the
Harshest thing known to us,"
Mumbles Shoo!

Blinded
—Kshirabdhi Tanaya Patra

Read about a thousand aphorisms
But am blinded,
Blinded by the way my soul unleashes
To your single touch,
Blinded by the way my mind finds solace
In your words.
The light doesn't break passing
The prism anymore,
The darkness stays but doesn't
Scare me anymore,
The rays in your gaze is with
What I am blinded now.
Blinded by the way you make me forget
That is dangerous,
Yes, being blind is dangerous.
Not knowing what is next to come
Is dangerous.
Yet I know this is beautiful,
Burning in fire is beautiful,
Falling from the peak is beautiful,
So, holding your hands and dying with you
Is also beautiful.

A Poem For The Ol-Chiki

—*Sokhen Tudu*
Translated from the Santhali
by Hansda Sowvendra Shekhar

The Bengali script in Bengal
The Odia script in Odisha
I do not know the Bengali script
You do not know the Odia script
Let us agree to one script for Santhali
The Ol-Chiki is our script

They write in the Roman somewhere
They write in the Devanagari at some places
I do not know the Roman script
You do not know the Devanagari script
One script will unite us all
The Ol-Chiki is our script

Dear writer, for how long will you
Write your language using
Someone else's script?
You are dividing our readers
You are making our publishers lose money
Let us all understand this
The Ol-Chiki is our script

One language, one Script
This is what will strengthen us Santhals
The talents of so many of us
Scattered for the want of one script
All of us Santhals, let us solve this script issue.

I Used To Have Hope And Crazy Dreams
—Nadia Krøjgaard Eriksen

What doesn't kill you
Makes you stronger, they say.
But that's a lie. A foolish lie.
I was clearly stronger in the past.
I used to have energy.
Enthusiasm.
Courage.
I used to have hope and crazy dreams.

Rejoice in change, they say.
But it's a lie. A damn lie.
I don't like her. The new me.
I am beaten.
More sensitive.
A fragile nerve.
I am unwillingly transcended.

We The Tolerant
—Nivedita N

We love our cows.
We love our goats.
We love our pigs.
We eat them and the grass and
Let mother earth be naked.

We love our Mumma,
We love our Dadaji.
We love our Chechi.
We feed them the curry served
From the palate of our mind.

We love our pistachio-flavored walls
And shield ourselves there.
We watch the news hour debates;
Fight with the ones we care.

We love You. We love Him.
We love Her. We love every Blank Space.
We love it? We are neutral. We love that?
Work in Progress.

We love the priest. Priestess?
Pin drop silence like silk-patch on our eyes
We love that neighbour across
Our hallway. But, down the street?
Rinse. Repeat.

We love we? You love you? I love me?
Forget it. Think later.
Let's go to the Machi Bazaar - taaza
Available in the supermarket.

A Plucked Flower
—*Arpita Subhadarshinee*

Oh! My little girl, with an archipelago of dreams,
The daddy's princess and the mother's pride,
Like an angelic sparkle and a priceless emerald,
With the biggest heart and an enlightened mind.

I remember those times together,
When swore we would spend time forever
I remember those smiles and fun,
One blink of eye and the past has gone.
You were fighting on a battle field,
You had lost your arms and weapons,
You were scared and defenseless.
Hoped that faith will come strong.

Fatal scars and tough weeks of battle
I thought nonsense were doctors,
Drips and medicines
Let cancer not win this fight,
Hopefull, it just remains a zodiac sign

She dies. I live. I cry.
The riddle called life, too difficult to handle
Love is so cruel.It makes us feel the pain,
I feel, the world has become a darker place
To dwell
Destiny had a different role to play
She left us to yearn in the midway
I laid beside on that hospital bed
Crying of hurt, coz few things left unsaid
The almighty made you His,
Journeys have bid us apart.
But am with you and you are with me
Always in our hearts.

Dear, I look at your empty bed
Still feel you are present beside me
This is not the end
I will see you out there in the middle someday
We weren't even friends. We were soul mates.
The soul sisters.

Gas Chamber
—Maria Pomsaharova

Sentenced to death row
In a gas chamber I sit
Breathing in memories
Of pain and sorrow
I suffocate while I cry
Falling down on the ground
Crawling towards the door
To discover I am locked out
By my inability
To forgive and forget all
What has been said and done

The Mad Poet's Refrain

—Lopa Banerjee

Poetry, the lump in my throat,
The bite sized chunks I gulp.
Like the thorny night that stings
The hysteric, brown earth,
Yet croaks in its own tainted lightning,
Words will find their way amid the rubble,
Relentless, beating, thumping.
Come home, to the potholes, bumps,
Step in the puddles of the folds
Between my palm, dear words,
As my neurotic mind squashes you,
Aborts you, again begets you.
Come, let me sip you with recycled juices,
Snatches of hogwash conversations.
I know you will come out some time
I will least expect, in spurts,
In malignant droplets,
In the edge of my waking.

Allegory For
Burning
—*Nabina Das*

Once it was known that
The arsonists were gone
The grass bloomed on the path
Of the walkers
My brother had friends who nearly
All got stoned
And he too, I think, just on ideas
Of identity and fun

All this scared the arsonists and
They were on the run
The men in the colony wore
Relaxed wear on streets
Once the arsonists were chased
Out of dreams
Our mothers cooked fish
And spread pickles in the sun

Once the cows were safe in the sheds
And lovers kissed
Their hands sought warmth,
Not the steel of knives
Grass seeds still soaked and
Gravel scented of bliss --
Nothing seemed less wondrous
Under those skies

When the arsonists came,
The cows were dozing
Their hooves sleepy and
Eyes perked to motion
A single flame was enough
To send the birds screech
The alleyways had started up
In a strange ashen flight

Our women were washing up
After lovemaking
The men were not sure
If they wanted a smoke
The boys thought someone burnt
Their dirty mags

The little girls were learning to
Compare not-breasts

It's the lovers in the shed
Who cried out loud at first
Grass pollen will be our eyes
And khorisa our tongues
And they cried and begged
To the kadamba of the night
In this story the arsonists had to go
Before the ruins

The arsonists stumbled over cinders,
They forgot names
Even the gods didn't help them
Retrace their sins
In this story our foremothers
Enjoy their primal lust
The men air themselves with the
Handfan and sleep
Everyone sings: we need warmth
We need flesh

The young girls learn saying
Love like a fruit one sucks
Even the boys agree to be high
On the sight of clouds
Give us fire
Give us wind
Give us water
Give us silence
Give us give us

They prayed till the arsonists
Were burnt in love

Keep Your Children Indoors For, The Barbarians Are Out

—Rajinder Arora

Keep your children indoors
Not just in Kashmir
But in every village
Town and city.

Don't send them to school
Or playground.
Don't read them a book
Or answer questions.

Don't let them speak
Or talk to them.
Don't lead them to truth
For lies abound.

Don't love them either,
Or talk of love.
Don't talk of life
Or the lives lost.

Don't let them think
Or raise a voice.
Don't. Just don't
Let a child be born.

The Taste Of Chasm Beneath My Feet

—Ipshita Sengupta

The Sunday afternoon,
Before your tongue split my lips
To make room for it inside my mouth,
I was dreaming of the sea.

How the receding waves
Leave behind a hollow under my feet.
Every time it hits me and goes back,
I sink a little deeper into the sand.

Eight seconds and six swirls
Of your tongue later
When you withdrew,
You left behind a familiar hollow.

Boys Don't Cry

—Shrideep Mohapatra

The day he was born,
Someone whispered in his ears
Boys don't cry.
All the emotions are to be swallowed.
Fed on the societies skewed version
Of masculinity,
All his emotions froze inside him.
As boys don't cry
All those beatings, heartbreaks
Were stuffed inside him,
As boys don't cry.
The blue-eyed girl was eventually
Disenchanted, as that boy finally
Bared his soul, and talked about
Feelings frozen in time.
As boys, dont cry.
Sometimes all those pent-up heart breaks,
Rejections, and suffering spilled
On the paper or in a glass of whisky.
As boys don't cry.

Only In India
—Kuffir Nalgundwar

Only in India could you start a study with this
Goal: 'the reluctance of the marginalized and
Vulnerable communities to send their children
To school', and still be considered liberal.
You might as well study their reluctance to stay
Away from jail, or their refusal to apply for Bail.

You'll be hailed by all as more touchable.

What would remain untouchable are questions
Like: why does the tightened noose, or the
Fired bullet, or the bucket filled with shit find
'The marginalized and vulnerable' so touchable?

Why is it so easily believable that the maid
Seduced the man of the house, or the slum
Fleeces the city, or the man bit the dog?

Some questions lack merit.

Like some village deities, they come alive only
When the rains arrive or when universities cut off
Anxious tongues. How is it that the sewers always
Open up when they reach the shanties,
Or the huts always bite the dust when a river is
Dammed? How is it that piped water can
Easily scale the tallest skyscrapers but never
Descends into the toilets in the slums down below?

Some questions lack merit.

But these are issues that need urgent scholarly
Attention: so many 'marginalized and
Vulnerable' babies give away their mothers to
Serfdom, and mothers give out their wombs;
So many girls save themselves for gods, and
Gods give them away to whole villages. And the
Immunity of disempowered communities
To good health? The high addiction to poverty
Among them and their propensity to embrace
Exploitation? So much to study.

The Difficulty
Of Childhood
—*Bijaya Biswal*

My five year old niece
Has too many complaints from life.

They're already teaching tables in Math class
Her bench-mate never returns her pencils
Games periods are short
Shoelaces tough to tie
Her lunchbox is getting predictable
She can never reach the top-shelves
Tooth-fairies aren't trustworthy
It's difficult to catch a butterfly.

She asks if life is hard only when you are a kid.
Adults never cry.
They have no reason to lie.
I wish I could tell her,
Broken crayons can still colour.
But broken human-beings
Only wait
To die.

That we haven't grown up.
We have grown out.

Bindusagar
—Abhishek Tripathy

Many souls meet
In an ocean of tranquilty
As mahalaya brings their kith
To its banks.
Like drops merge to create
This ocean of devotion.

Ananta Vasudeva and
Lingaraja temples
Reflect in your flow,
With chandan yatra and
Chapa khela of the Lords…
Generations have seen you
Like a mirror of their times
From ancient sages
To modern ways.

The soothing aroma
From the temples' kitchens
Invite a vigorous engagement
With the gastronomic delights.
Many tourists, and as many priests,
Vie for attention, of each other
And the lords'!

The lotus blooms add
Charm to the banks,
And as night sets many lights
Glow along the road.
Serene, and at peace,
Bindusagar, your journey flows.

Bare And Lonely

—*Anup Narayanan*

Bare and lonely,
Abandoned by my muse,
And in God's own country,
June skies without nimbus.

The Moon
—*Nava Anup*

The moon is awake tonight,
The moon is shining bright!
It's a really beautiful sight,
The waves by the sea is quiet!
As the night gets pleasant,
The moon is a crescent!

Mr. Stranger
—Pritam Laskar

Dearest stranger,
How long have you been waiting here,
Sipping stale coffee,
Listening to others' songs clawing out
Of the dilapidated jukebox; whilst you,
Enlightened one, live in fear
Of the imagined aliens and
All-knowing almighty, and shout
Slogans silently whispered in your ear
By well-dressed sheep?
Tell me, wanderer, how long till you figure out
That the price
Of not resisting the piper as he fakes promises
And weeps
Crocodile tears into his velvet handkerchief,
Sending crowds into cries
And shrieks of inconsolable grief,
Is more than what you will pay
If you listen to your mind and think
What you really want to say?

For The Solace Of
Undead Things
—*Kartik Thopalli*

Fault lines
Straining across the palm
Follow along the margins
To the floral familiarity
Of spring opening
To the undemanding light
Of a derelict repose of the
Battered city
And its people.

The geography of sorrow
Cannot be traced onto a map
Her desecrated smile
Is everything
The apex of the unflinching north.

Withstanding the
Oppression, the river
Trudging across the naked earth
Has carried her decadence
And somewhere in its course
It has carried mine.
In the glimpse of an obliviated dream
The delicate politics
Of corrupted love is purged.

Your Shits Will Not Be Normal

—Sumeet Samos

Our daily walks of shit,
We searched for the thickest of Bush
To hide behind,
Dry dust rubbed with the left hand,
We poured some water from the
Half broken bottle.
Men by 6 and women by early 4:30 lest
The sun light appears,
From dust, ash, soap to handwash
Is how my life changed.
Women's walk to night shit
Was always in groups,
Filled with a sense of immense fear.
Fear of armed men with green clothes
By the riverside camp,
Molestation by these green snakes
Had been frequent by then.

Our daily walks of shit,
Their one step behind the house shit,
Left behind with flies all over them
Early morning,
Brooms on their hands,
No expression of your ewwwwww,
With no masks went some from my basti,
Your shit equalled to 5 Rupees of our
Basti's BPL subsidized rice.
Shit was the everyday normal,
So normal that eyes staring
At it for minutes evoked no emotions nor
Provoked the senses.

All types of shit throughout the day,
Gandhi's village republic was in full power here.
First time latrine was a mobility,
Anything outside the village seemed mobility.
From manual scavengers, bonded laborers to
Any work in towns and cities seemed mobility,
From bare feet, paragon, to shoes now is mobility,
From eating rice and boiled tamarind juice
To eating extra subjis is mobility.
This doesn't stop here,
Will strive for as much comforts in life.

Romanticizing village is
One of the biggest shit,
Na jal mera, na jangal mera,
Na Zameen mera,
We are just a demarcating line
In the village for you to unload
Your heaps of shit.
Spread the news from village to universities,
Your shits anywhere will not be
The normal anymore.

Bohemian Soul
—Sufia Khatoon

I drift and I wander
Not in soil or sky,
But in sound and silence.

A mind full of adventurous dreams,
Sits quietly relishing the peaceful moments
After every breath of monotonous city air.
A corner of a room that opens to the sky,
A big window of wind chimes singing
Yesteryear's melodies.
I shall be travelling soon without me
To find me again.

I hold tomorrow and today,
Not to be invisible but to stay closer
To the bohemian in me.

Wildest spirits and unquenchable thirst
To know the uncertain,
To walk through the solid curtains,
And be there in that moment silently
Uniting with the universal power.

The Big Barn Owl
—Tanuja Sethi

A big barn owl sitting on a tree
Chin-chin ki-ki, the babblers got angry
"It's our home!" said one little bird
And curiously asked, "from where did
You come?"

Owl, "I'm old and lost and half-blind.
Do not shoo me away, if you'll be kind.
Please let me stay here, up in your tree,
I'll be a good bird, you'll see!"

There came a treepie, asking the same.
We are worried for our nests,
The babblers explained.

The Babblers were kind

Oh dear birds, please! I have nowhere to go,
The owl said.
After some debate and thoughts,
A deal was made.

The owl was staying

With the crescent moon, the night came by,
All slept peacefully, the babblers and treepies.
At dawn, the little birds saw empty nests
All they saw was the big barn owl fly.

Lo and behold
The owl was really old
So he played little tricks
As we were told

Romantics Are
A Dying Breed
—Eureka Alphonso

There are few who love life.
Fewer who live it.
But there are those
Who are consumed by it.
They find joy in small plants,
Growing from a cracked wall,
Or the fluttering wings of a butterfly.
Who appreciate soft fragrances.
Who are in love with the idea of love.
Who taste wine and gaze into eyes.
Who laze in the sun and smile at strangers.
Who enjoy conversations about the universe
And seek solitude in a crowd.
Who indulge in old books and
Walk barefoot on beaches.
Who admire flaws and praise beauty.
Who kiss deeply and breathe slowly.
Who laugh heartily and cry profusely.
Who care madly and dream daily.
These are the romantics of the world.
Who give us art, cinema and
Music from their soul.
Cherish them,
For they are a dying breed.

Whimsical Winds
—Tapan Jena

Strange whimsical winds,
Drifting across the city by lanes;
As if some poet's nomadic dreams.

Whether it's gloomy nights
Or bright mornings,
Winds won't stop;
As it can't differentiate these things.

Storming through the strange alleys,
There's none so place
Which stays windless.

Whether roaring blizzard
Or soothing breeze,
It pierce people's soul with
Discriminating ease.

In half agony and half hope,
I looked back and forth,
Could not get a glimpse
Of you in this unseen natural wrath.

Uncertain of my fate; I must depart,
To find you in my lonely heart.

Hairouna
—Jeon Julien

Every marning me get up
Me thank God for a new day
Dat me faculties still in order
With each passing day

Me look pon me pikney them
Some gone, while some stay
Me want all ah them be productive
But some want easy way!

Some does abuse and steal from me,
Extract all me goods from me pantry
While others want the betterment of de country

Yo does often hear them say
"Wha ah happen in Vincy today?"
If yo look good, yo go find wha wrong …..
We nah live according to the Almighty plan!!!

Love

—Rochelle Potkar

Late in the evenings when the forest grew sounds,
The smell of rain on dung, jungle of danger,
He kept arsenal in green -
Raw blood and just-alive meat.

A man with a heart - he loved animals.
Off a spinning hunt and new game,
He watched them through his binoculars.

The forest guards sleeping…

A leopard played with a boy's carcass
Through his camera-on-terrain.
He killed it in spite, roasted and ate it.
No dogs came near him after that.
An unusual smell coming off him.

The forest guards, sleeping…

A forest official once asked for buffalo horn,
Sent him to kill bovine.
He killed its baby too,
His head and stomach churning.
Until came a new forest-range officer,
Who told him of the role of every
Animal in the ecosystem.

He gave up hunting, and began
Tranquilizing rogue elephants
For a living.

But when it rained,
The gates of the forest broke.
Villagers turned away by floods
Became hunters and poachers again,
Like him.

They wouldn't have gone to danger
But forest-protection officials
Grew hungry
For a taste of rare meat
Every now and then.

Waiting
—*Sujit Prasad*

Now that maa is gone, sometimes
I want to ask my father what has been
His most abiding happiness
But then I fear

What if he does not say your mother,
Or the children, or that time we missed
The train together and found
The ocean still waiting for us?

What if he says he is still waiting?

The Mystery Of The Forest Bamboos

—*Jacinta Kerketta*
Translated from the Hindi by
Bhumika Chawla-D'Souza,
Vijay Chhabra
and
Fr. Cyprian Ekka

As I lay in the Kuruwa field in sweet slumber
I felt the earth beneath quake and tremor.
And I saw on the sweeping claws of an excavator
My field from its very roots severed.
On that machine hung
Not just that piece of land, but I as well,
And I realised then
The agony of being uprooted from one's soil.

The body of my ancestors
Was being rent and dismembered,
And I watched the pieces sell for millions.
The crowd of buyers
Turned into a teeming multitude,
And I felt as if my own body
Were torn into a million pieces and sold.

At the foothills of mountains
The new generations
Sell off their bamboos to ensure a secure future.
Breaking free from the machine claws
I picked up a bamboo and swore,
These bamboos shall go to the market no more,
In the forests they will remain this time
And become bows and arrows for each hand.

And then for the first time
The mystery revealed itself
Of countless bamboos lining the hills
And nurtured by ancestors with their very blood.

This poem was first published in Angor by Adivaani in 2016.

Rejected Poem
—Ajmal Khan

The poem was declared
As anti national and rejected
Like a US visa applicant
From Muslim country
It wanted to prove as nationalist
It started with Vande matharam
The continuing lines were only nouns
Of the independence struggles
In which the poem was part of
Rest of the lines were written in Green,
White and Kesari in color
Signed on the lines which start with J&K
That they are integral part
It ended with national anthem
The poem was again rejected
On the grounds
It had two names Hyder Ali and
Tipu Sultan in the foot note
Syntax had no saffron and khaki pattern
Moplah rebellion is included as one line
And instead of 1947 its written Azaadi.

Style
—Michael Creighton

On the east side of Africa Avenue,
Above the Nissan showroom,

Sits the Hotel Empire Deluxe.
It has no doorman and boasts no stars,

But there's an AC in every window—
And a bus stop one block over.

Let's get a room some afternoon,
And pretend we're sinning in style.

You Cannot Die, Manu Tanti

—*Gurinder Azad*
Translated from the Hindi
by Akshay Pathak

I kept silent at your death
Didn't speak with anyone either then yesterday,
Just across the metro when I spotted
A crowd of daily wage labourers
The thought of you came flashing;
In their faces I searched for the elegy to what
Followed your four days of labour..
But I kept walking, didn't stay there for long
Sometimes, the slogans to demand our rights
And your screams ground in that thresher-
Both seemed the same to my mind.
And sometimes my conscience drenched in fear
After looking at a vacuum appear on the vast
Backdrop of our movement;
Then giving myself false assurances, I moved
On your last few pictures on facebook, I have
Not been able to look at those.
But that image that moves faster than
Imagination, it disappears somewhere after
Witnessing your helpless last moments at the
Unknown shores of your family's remorse
But even in this the memory throws forth
However hazily, the vast backdrop of our
Movement where khairalanji and other such
Massacares appear holding on to canvases
However-
Manu Tanti knowing my conscience in
Whatever form..
Today, I shall speak with my broken, perhaps
Dwarf-like words that the time will change
Your circumstances your condition the news
Of your murder-
All have passed on to our marching feet
Our massacres/tragedies do not die!
And this isn't about demanding your wage for
Those four days of labour;
This is the balance of many centuries..
Till it is settled,
You cannot die, Manu Tanti!

Focus
—*Ramiz Shaikh*

Two round and juicy,
Chipper and sitting tight,
A must-glance arises,
After figuring out sizes.
Grub not too bad,
Bill looks upsetting,
But that dress,
Leaves the mind at rest.
Peeking while you peek,
Quietly suffocating,
Imagine them wild, free,
So much glee.
Time's up, home awaits,
That's all for two of the greats.

The Wait
—Mukul Soni

Two hours made
Two months look feeble

The heartbeat took leaps
With every careful and slow step
Under the amber light

A dog on the street,
Rusty store shutters and
The moon in the sky,
No one could comprehend the
Enormity of the moment

That moment when I found
Warmth in your fragrance

Notes